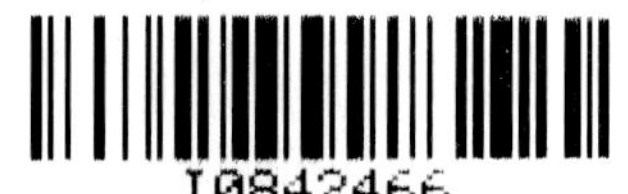

Beautiful Cabins

An Adult Coloring Book

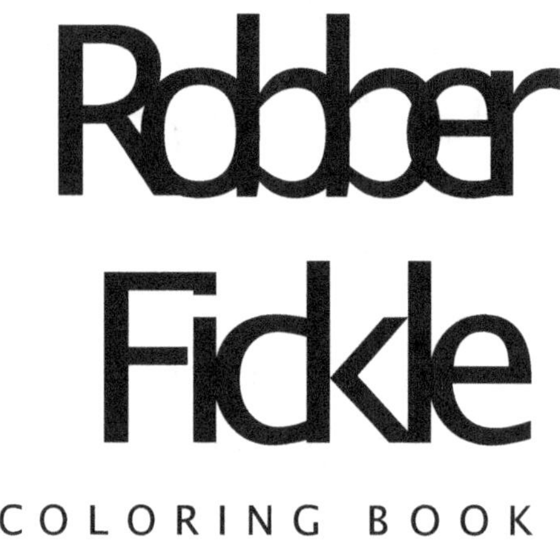

For Any Question and Suggestions
robberfickle@gmail.com

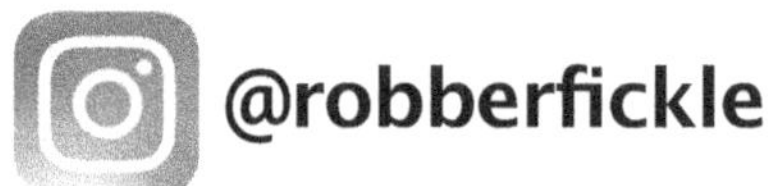 **@robberfickle**

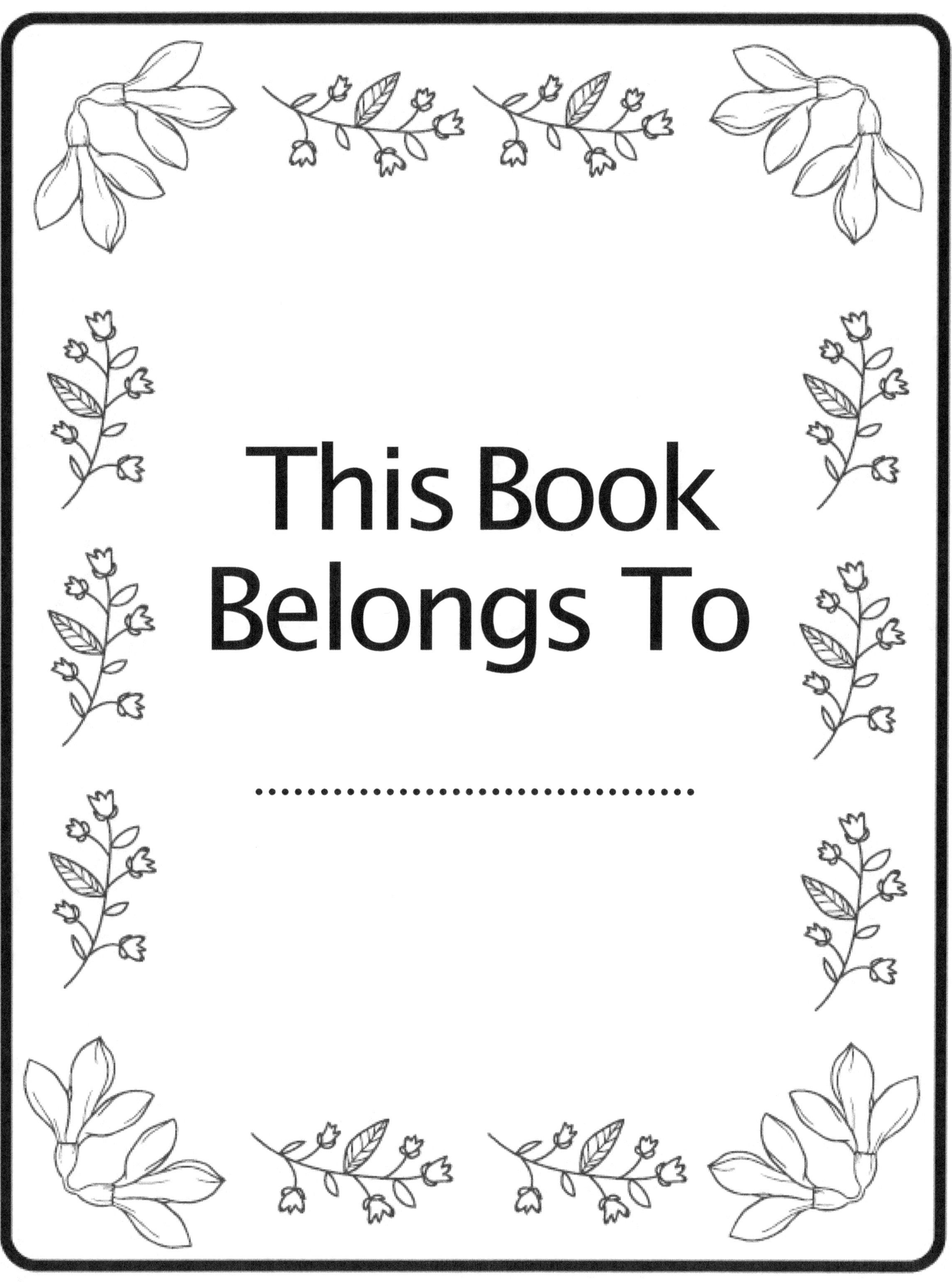

This Book
Belongs To

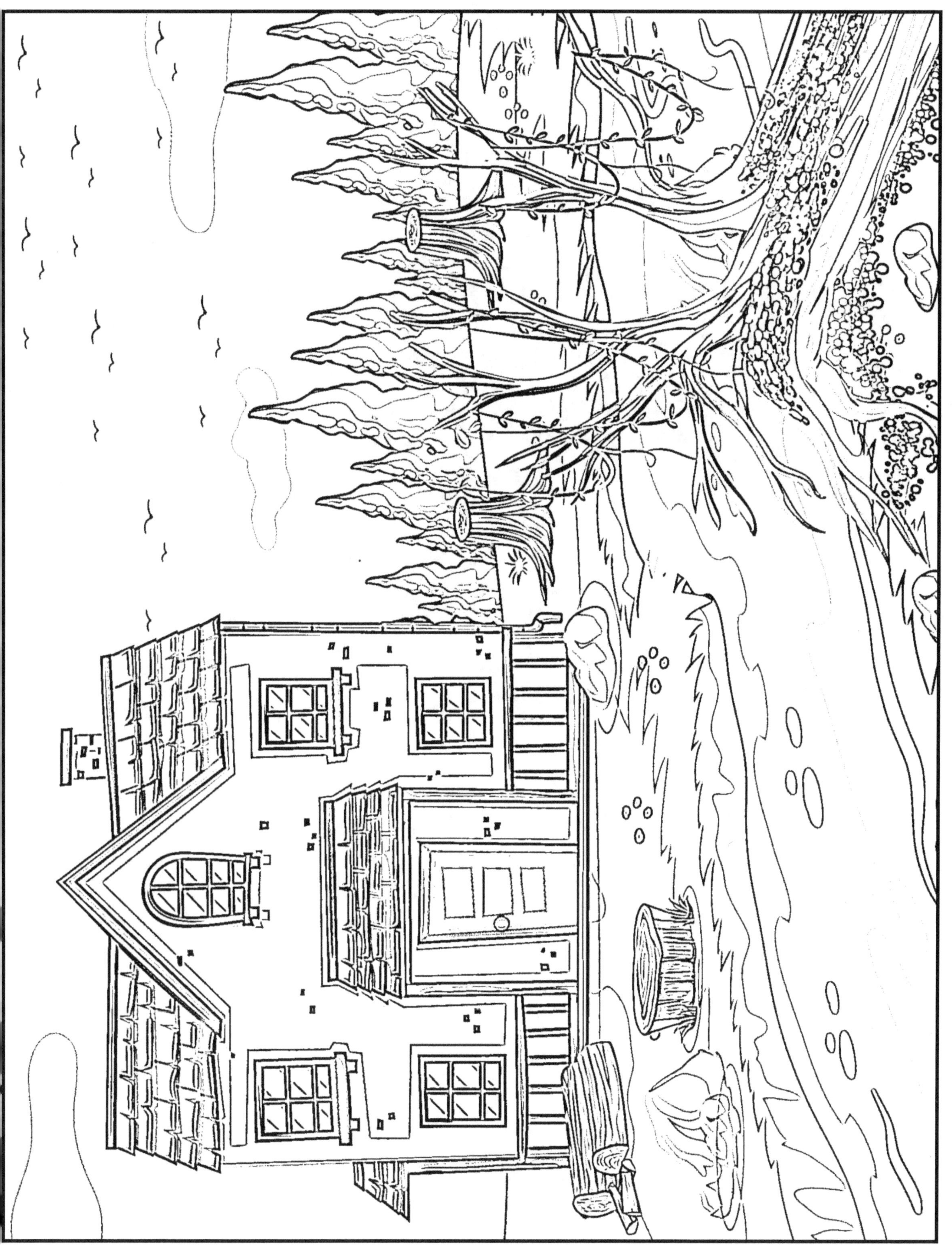

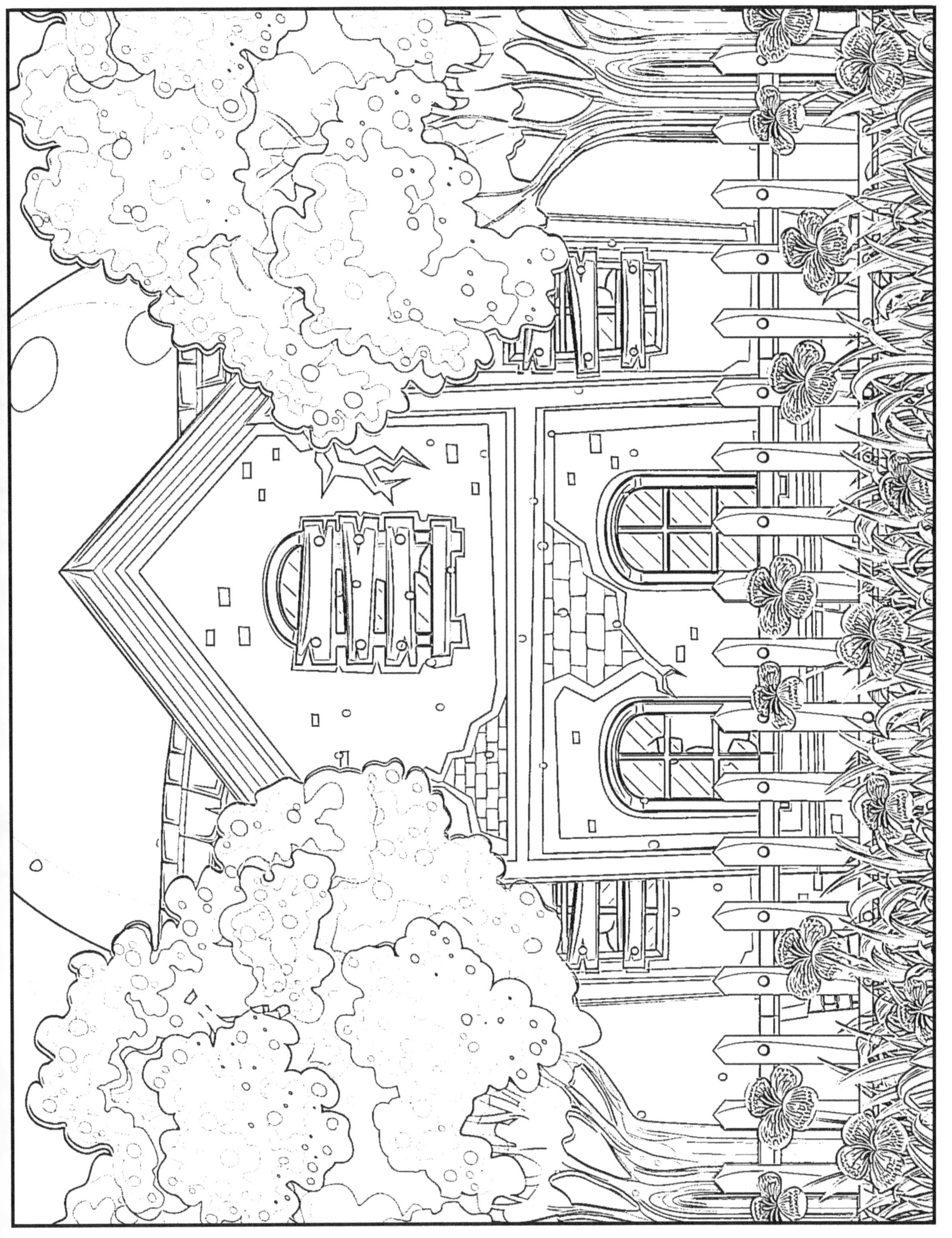

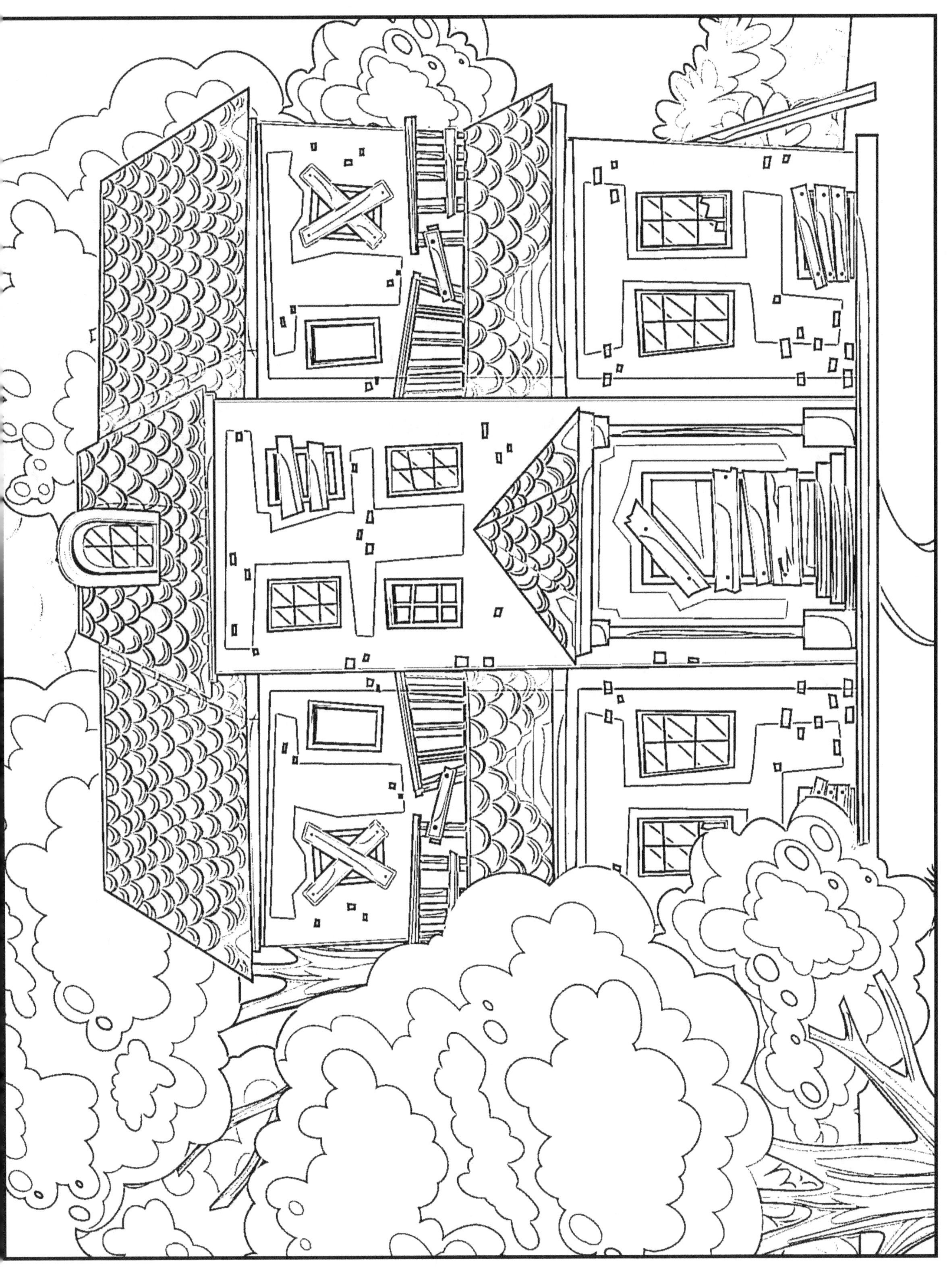

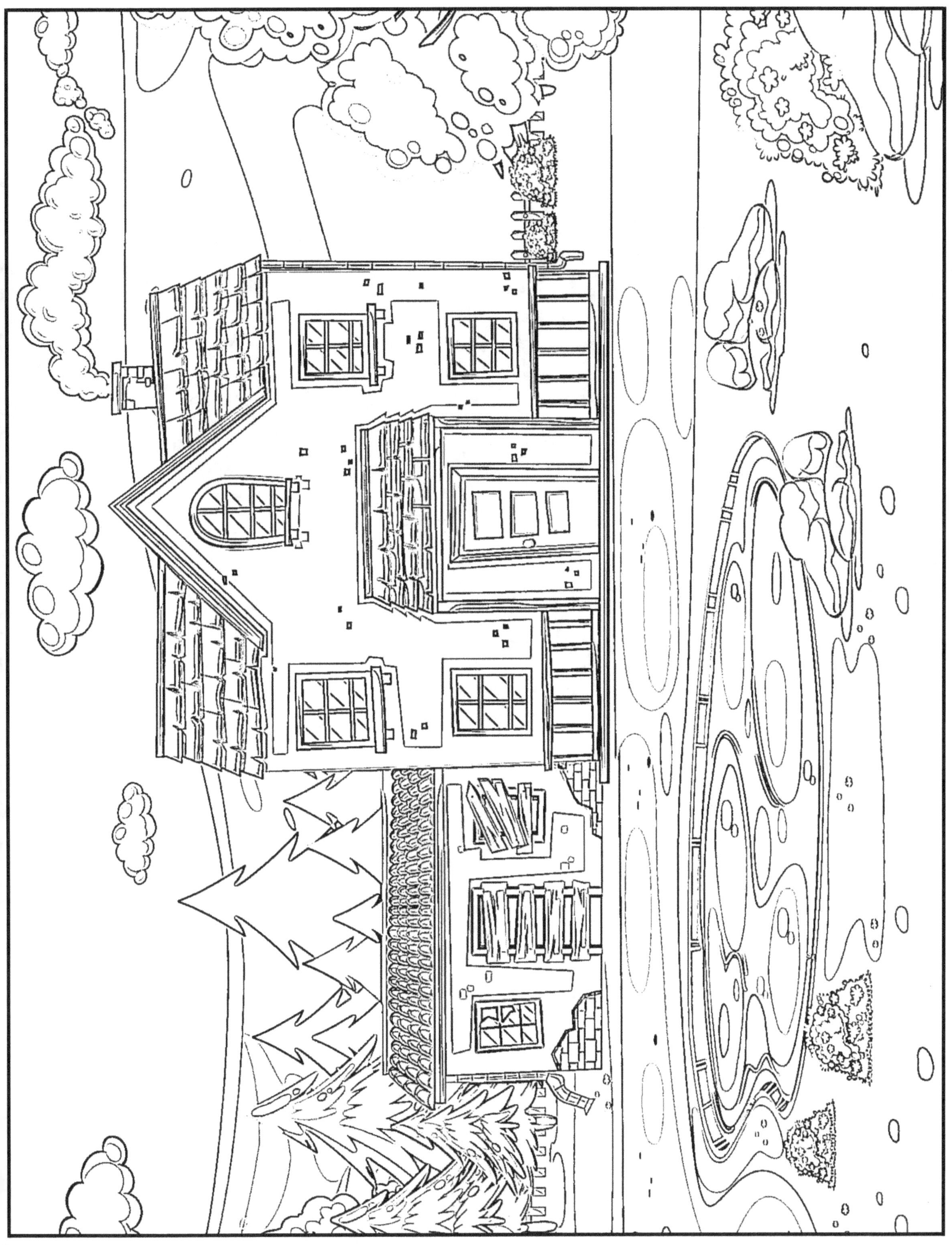

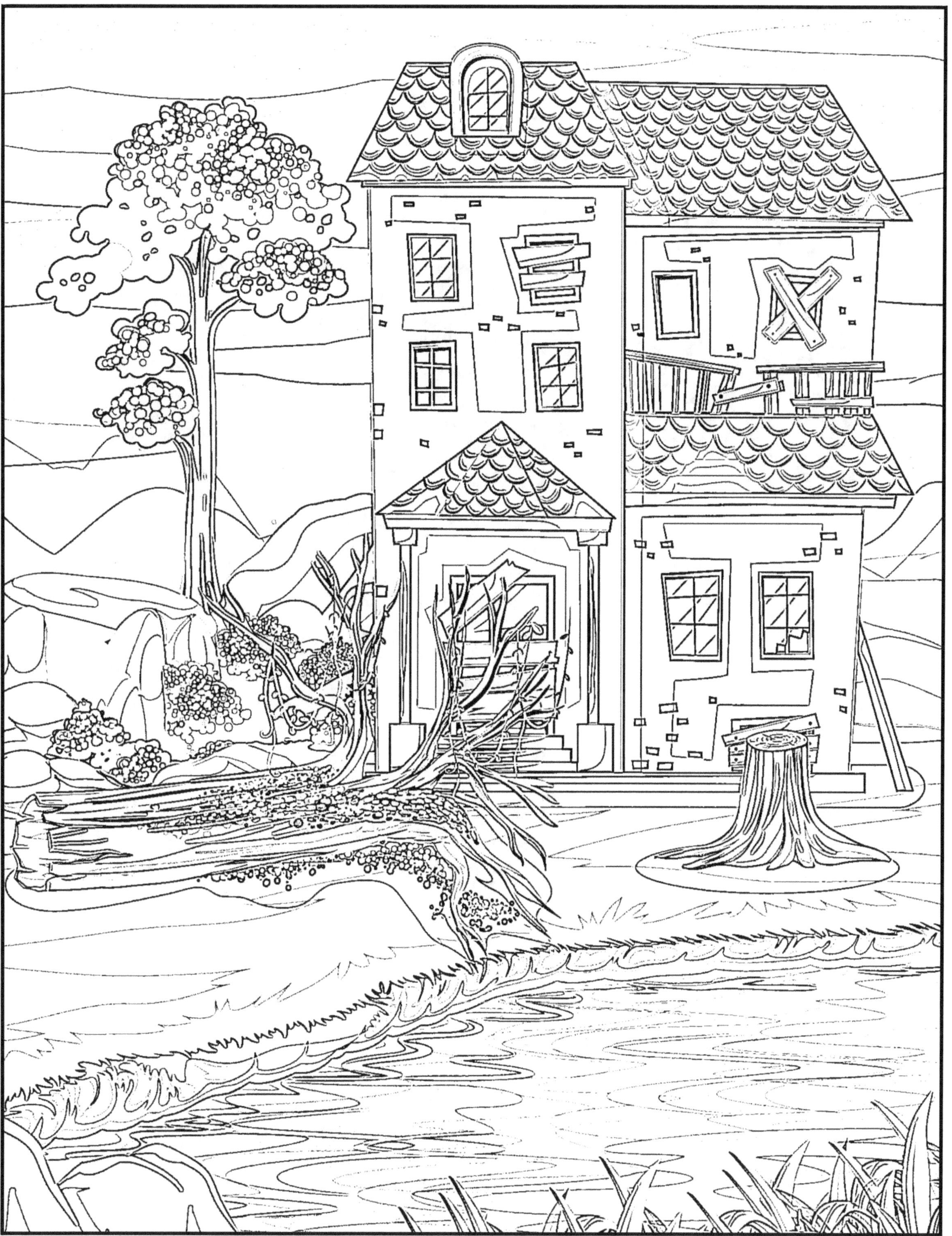

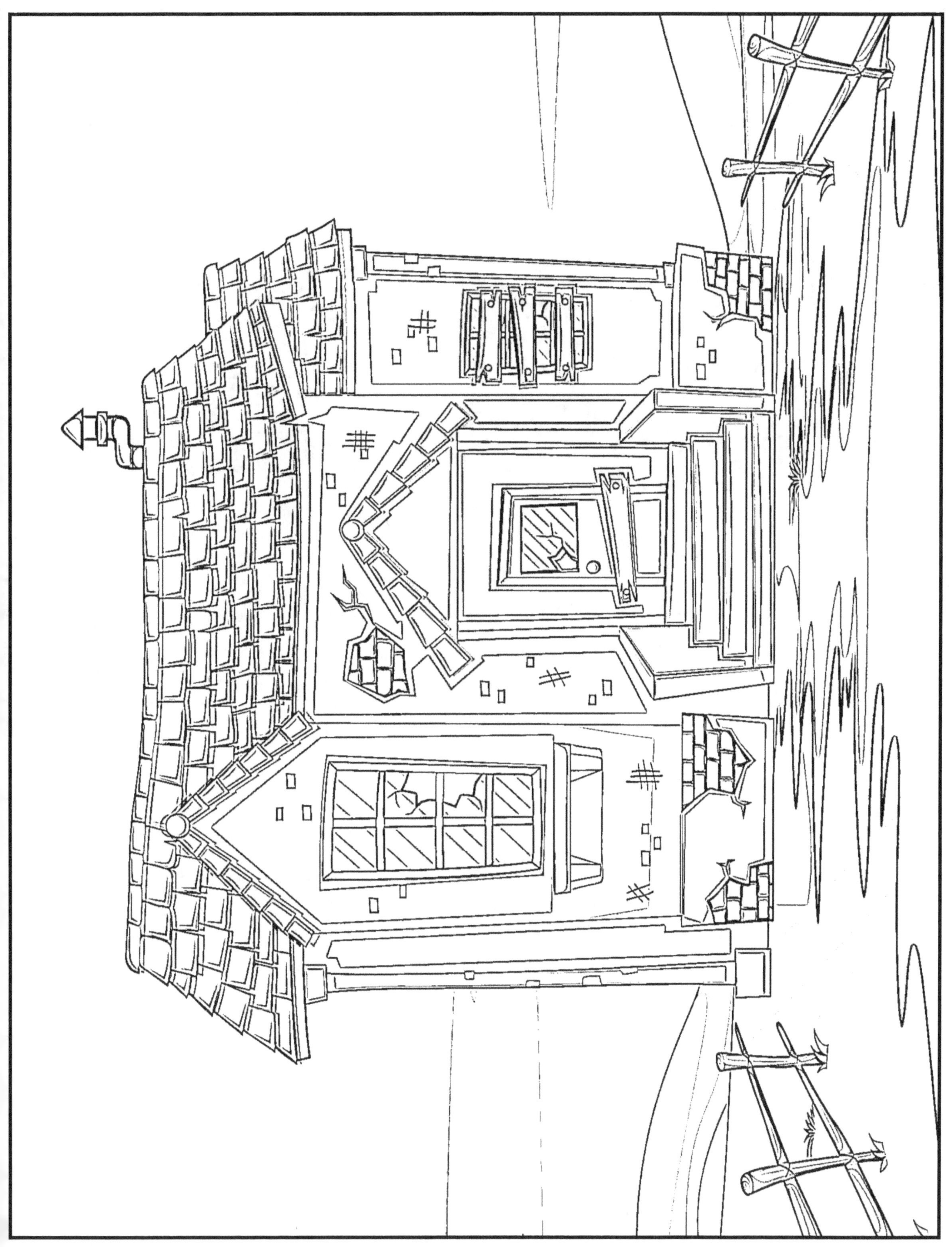

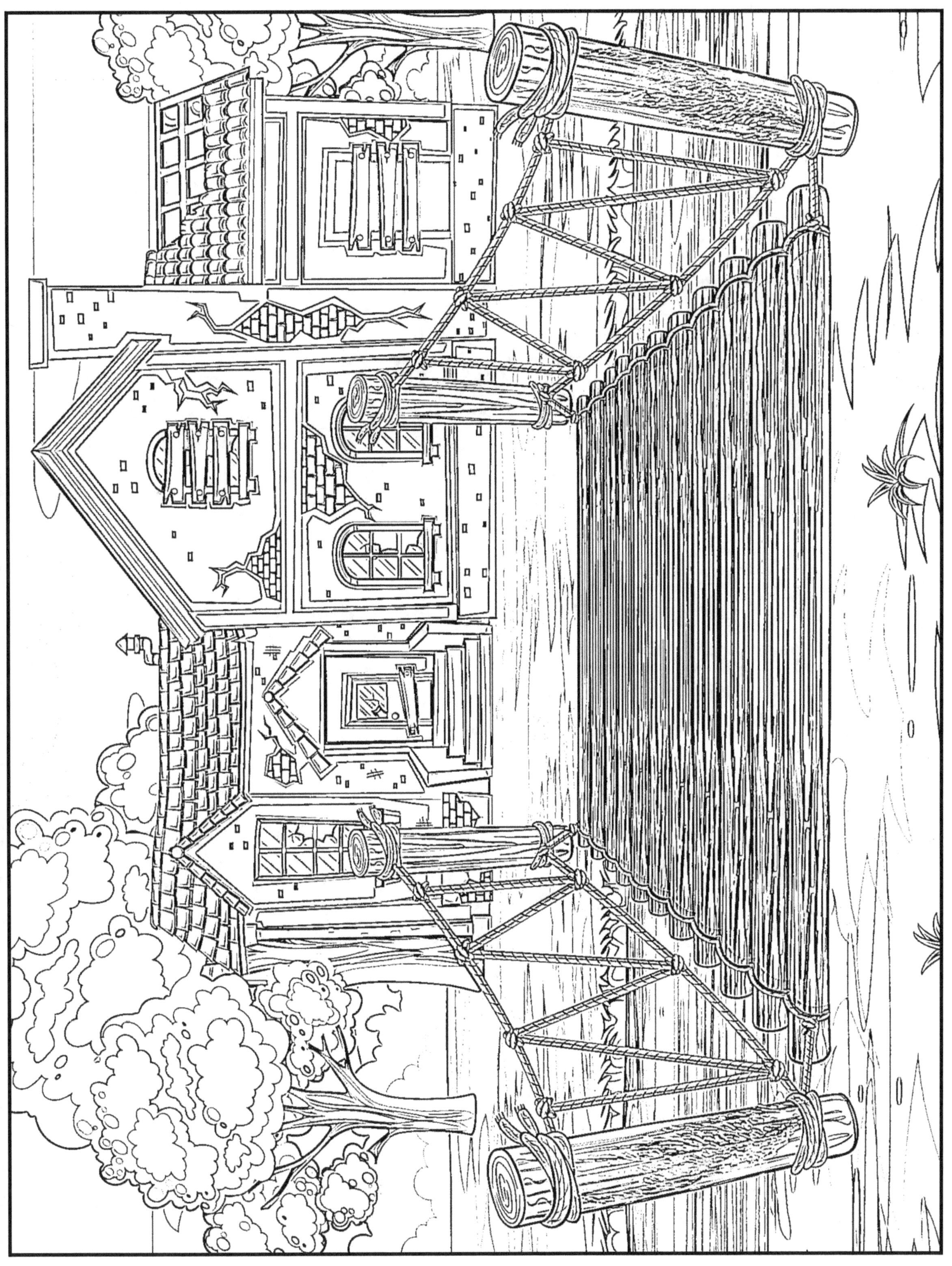

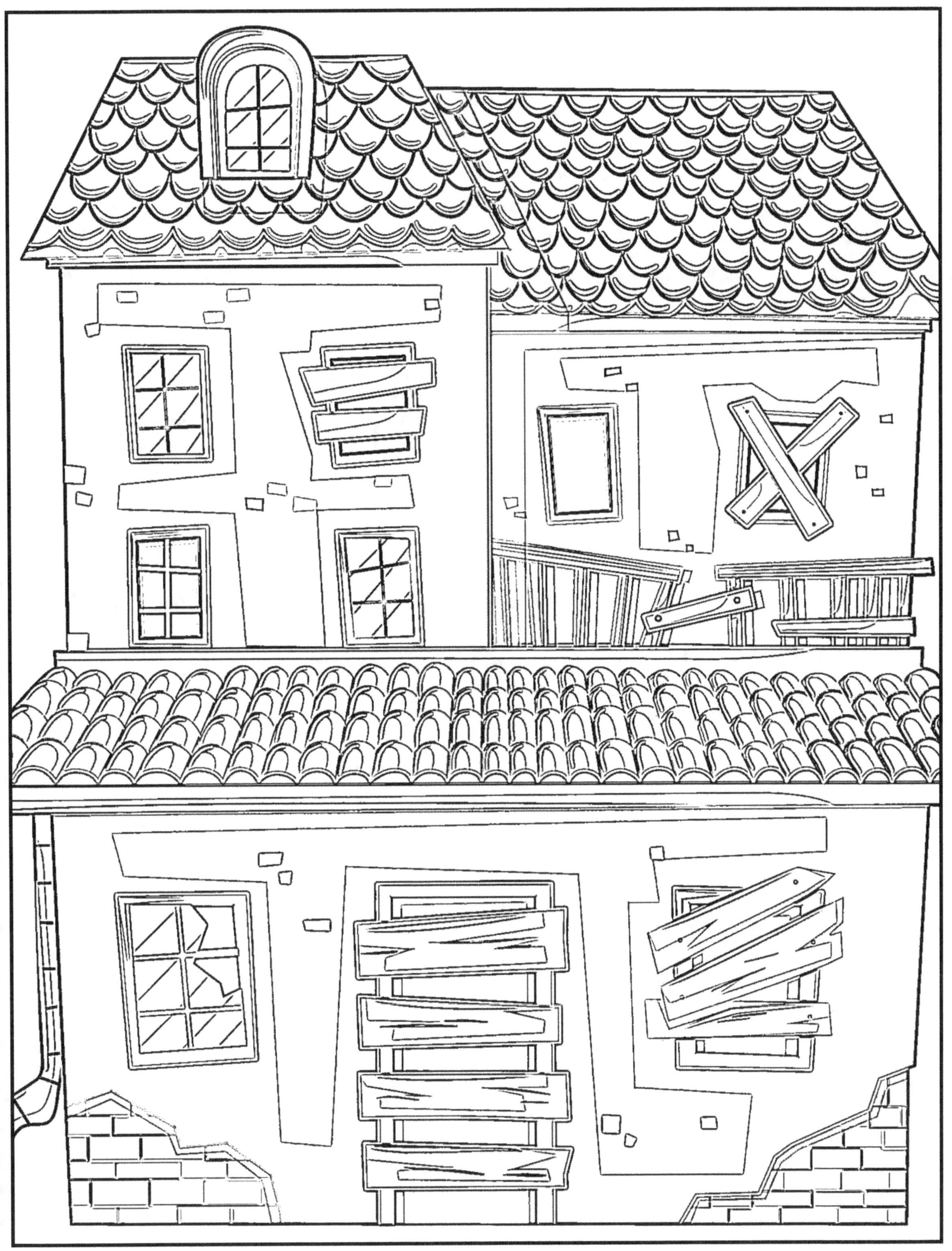

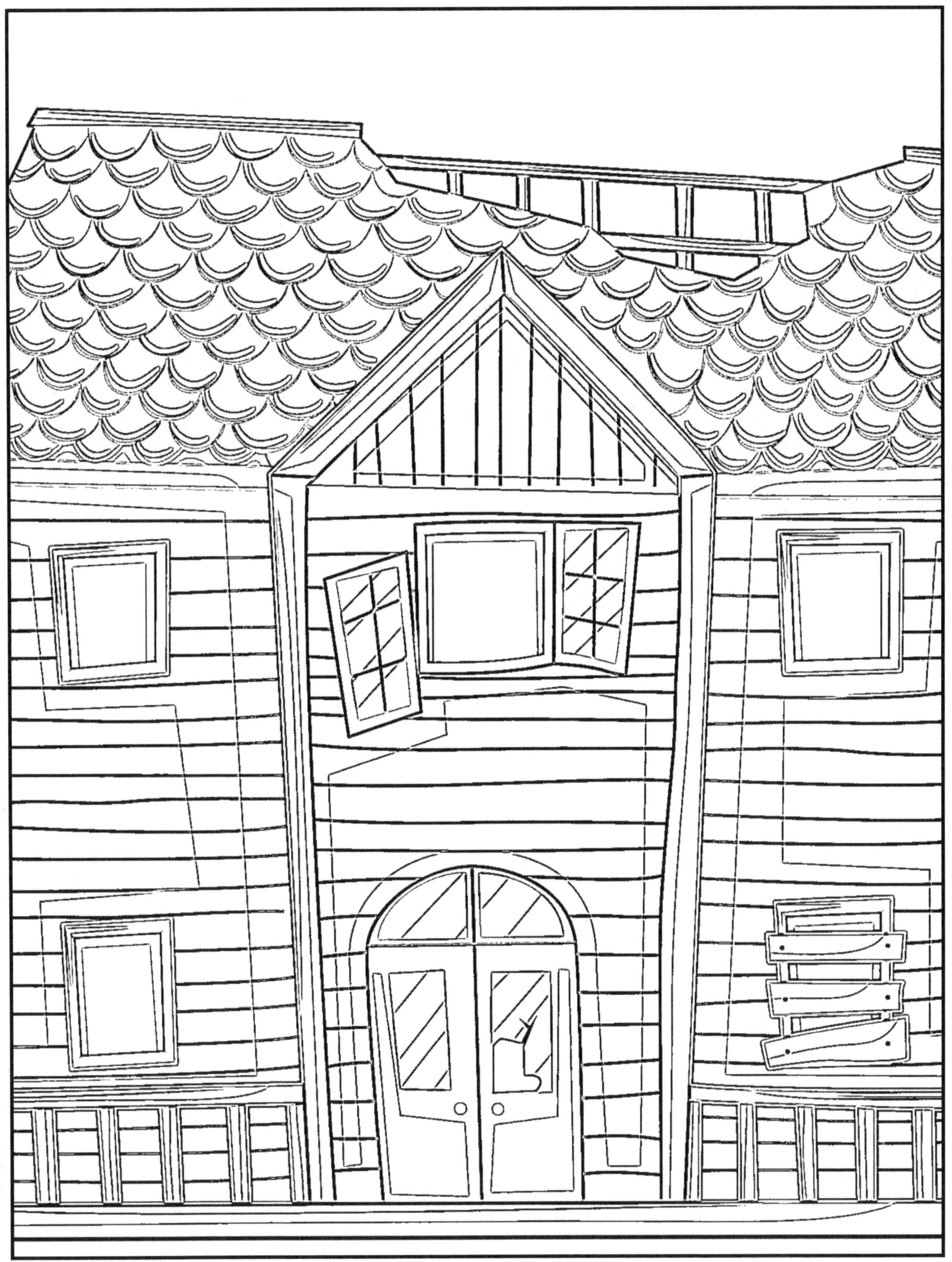

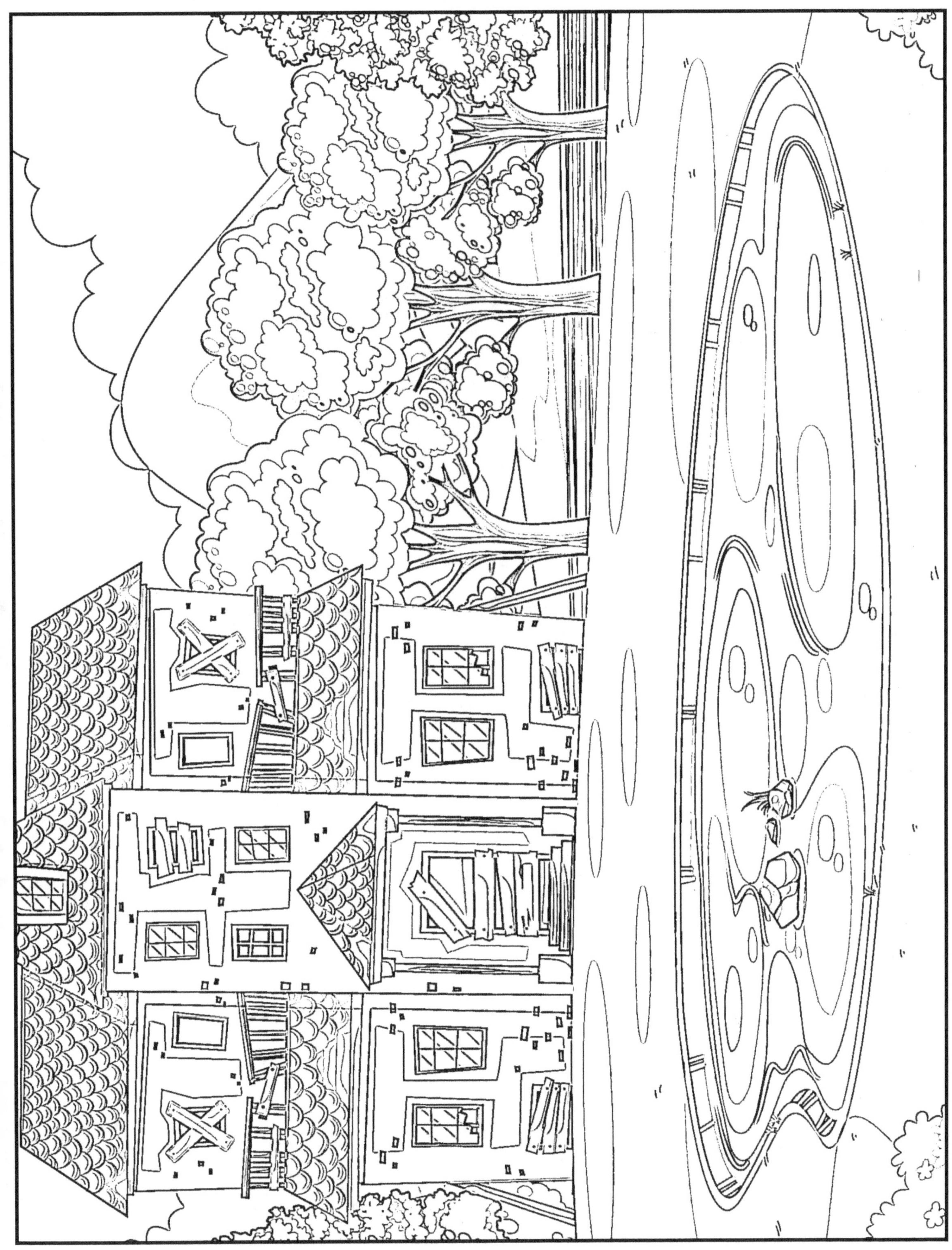

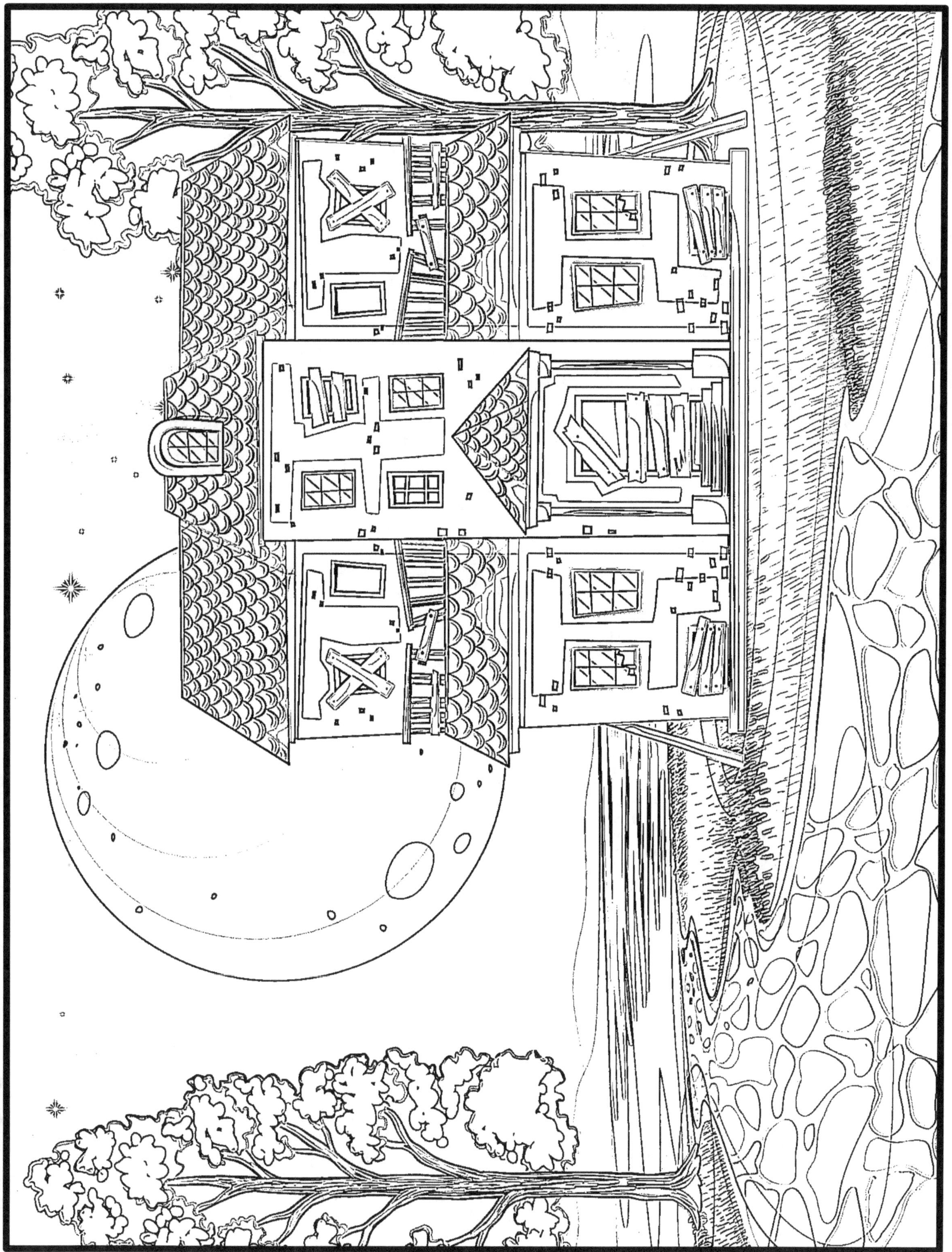

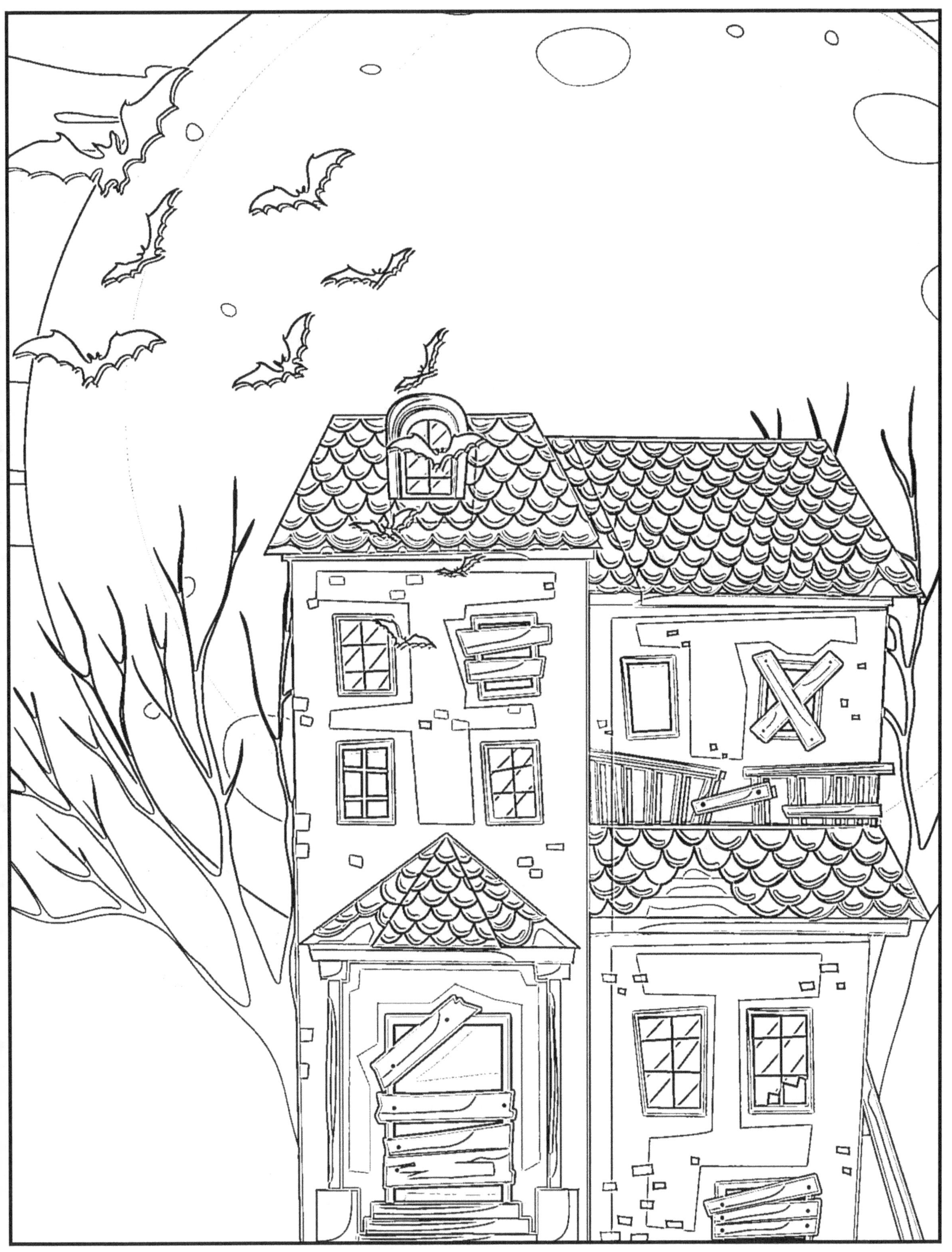

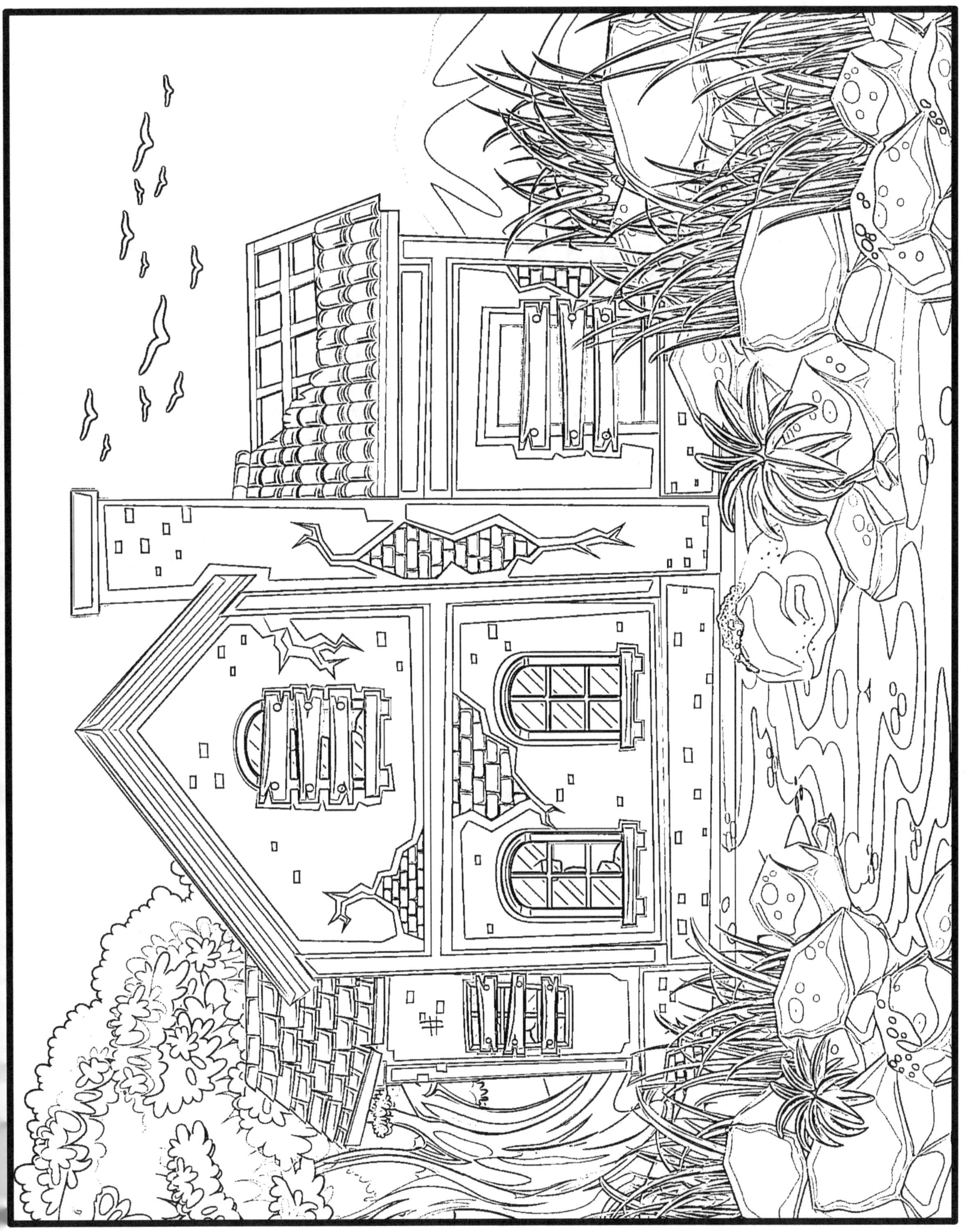

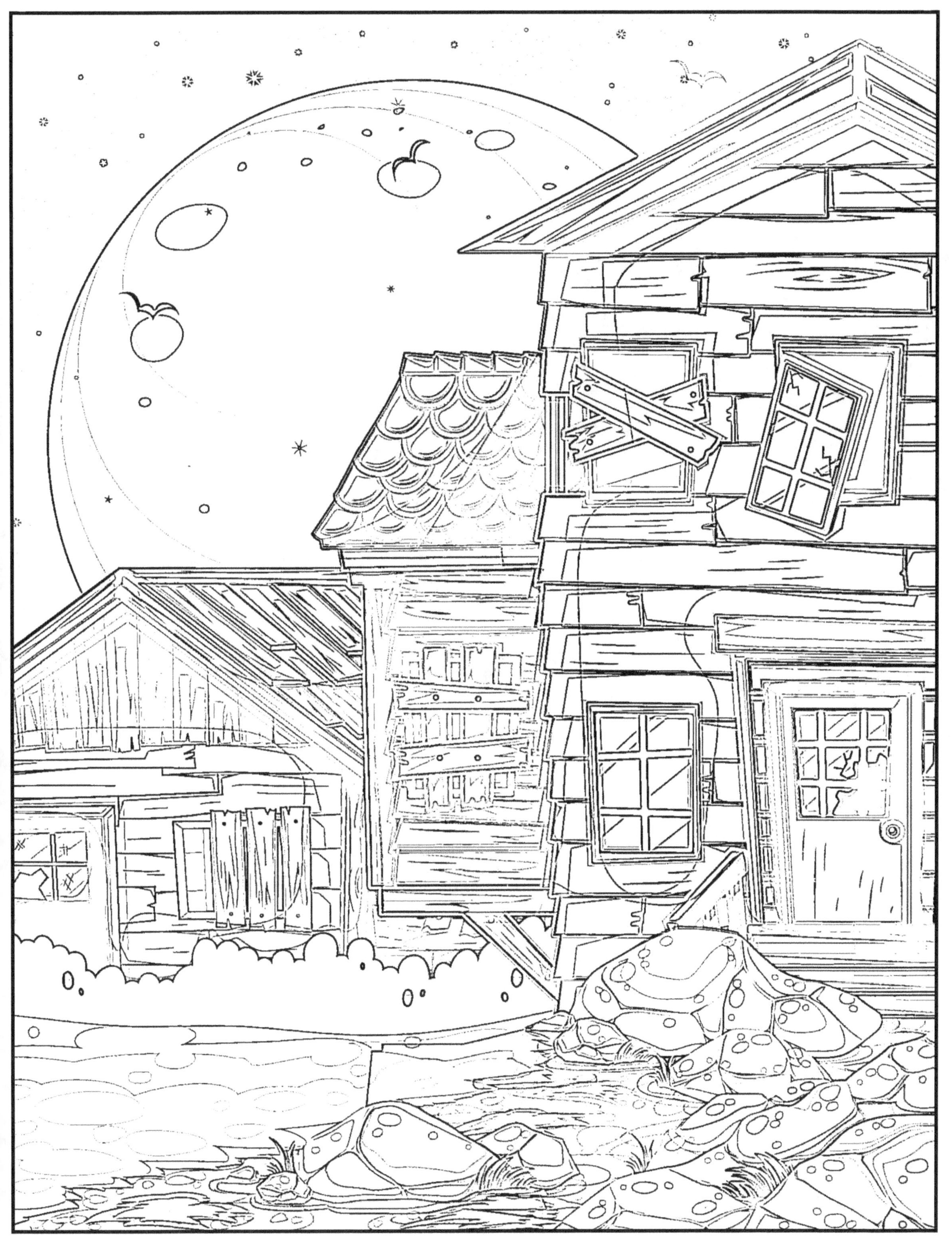

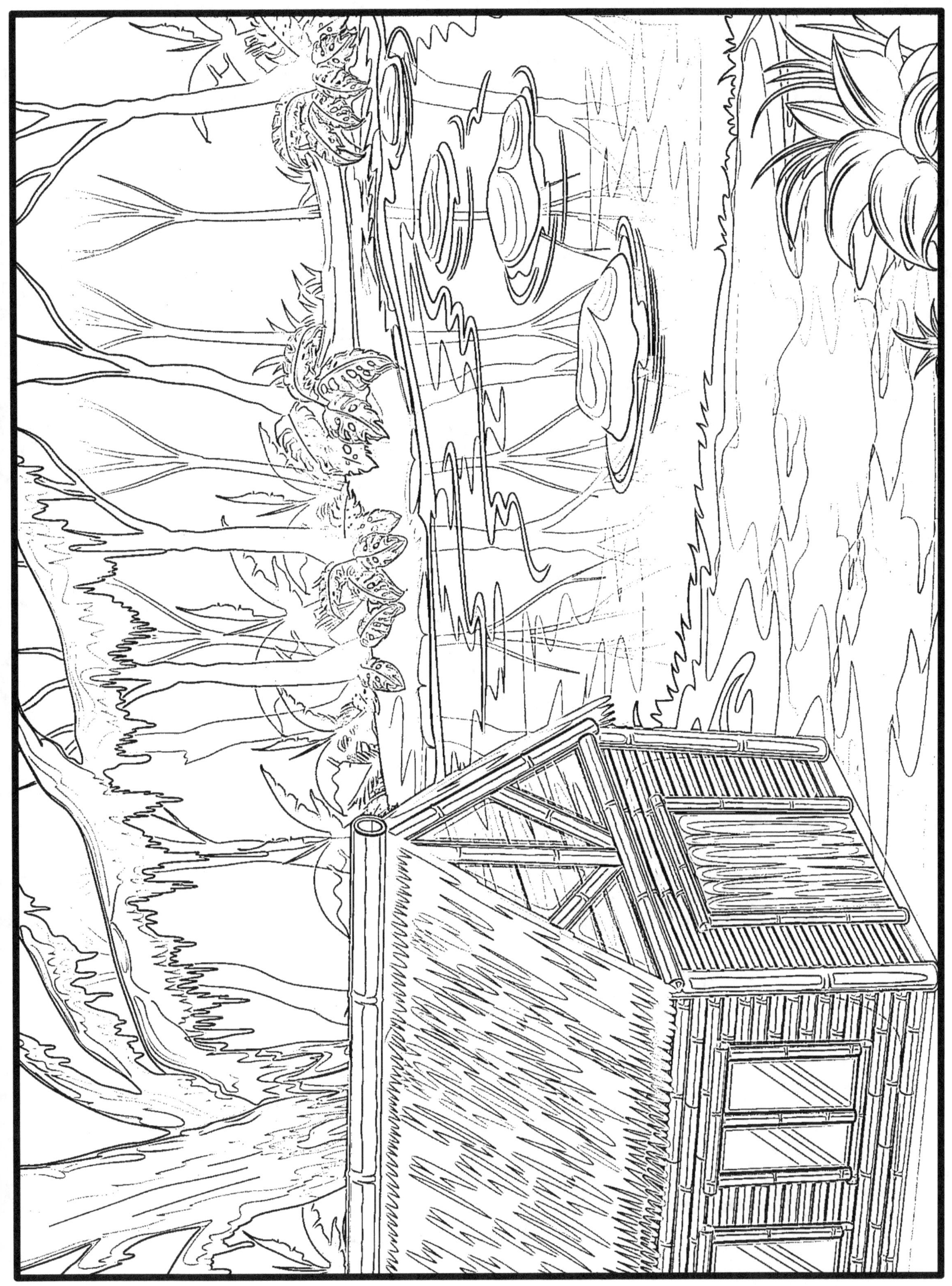

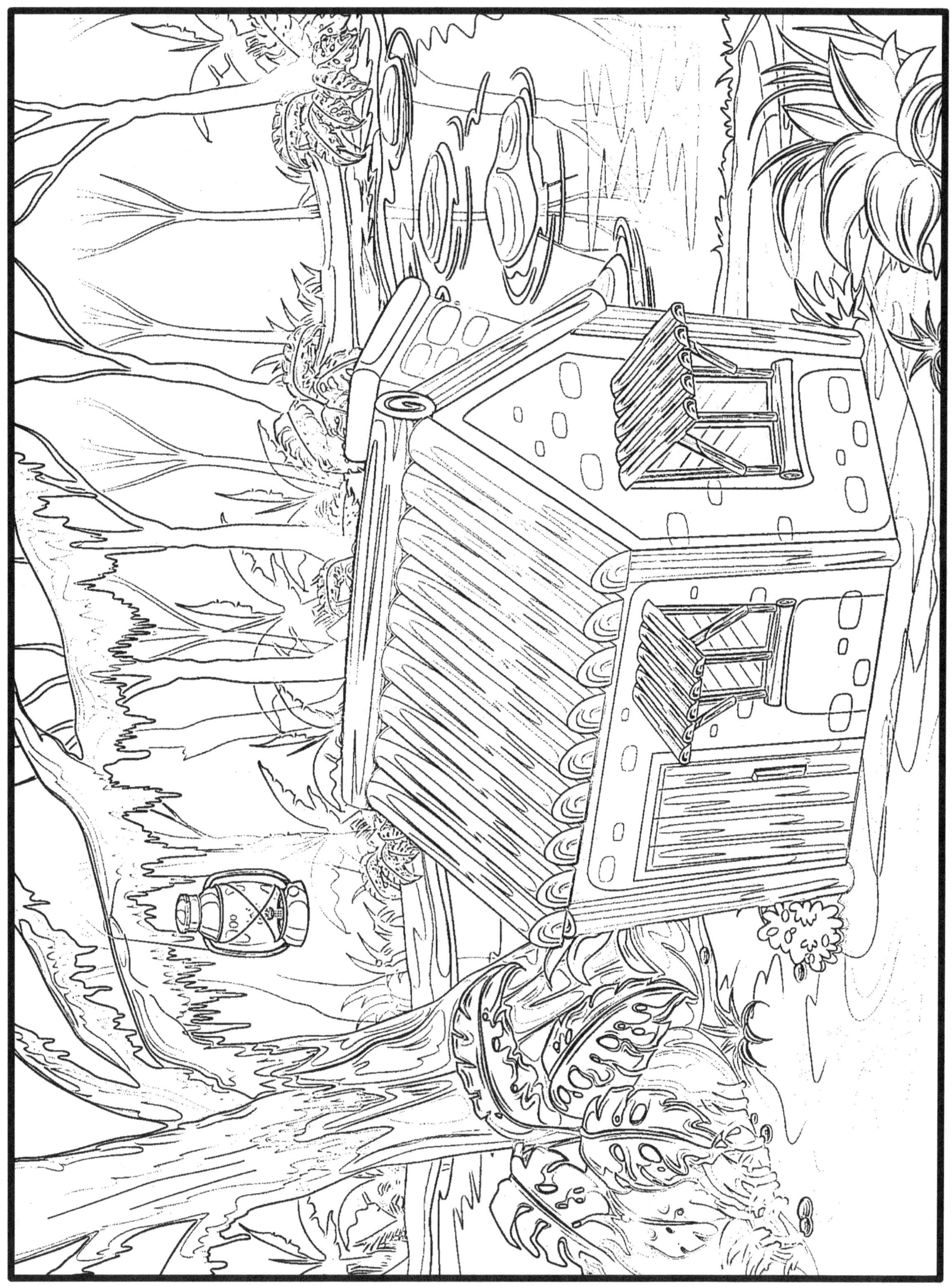

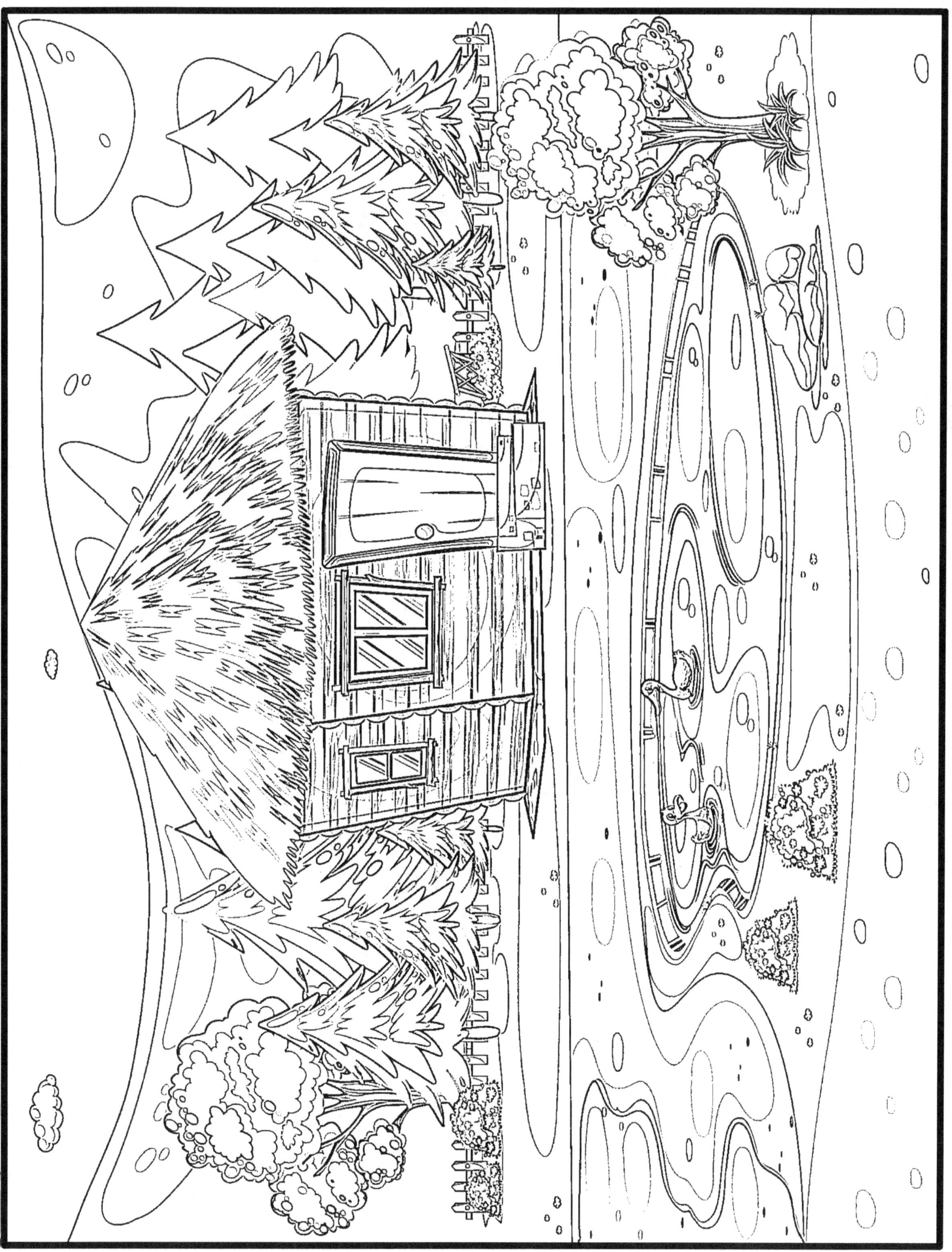

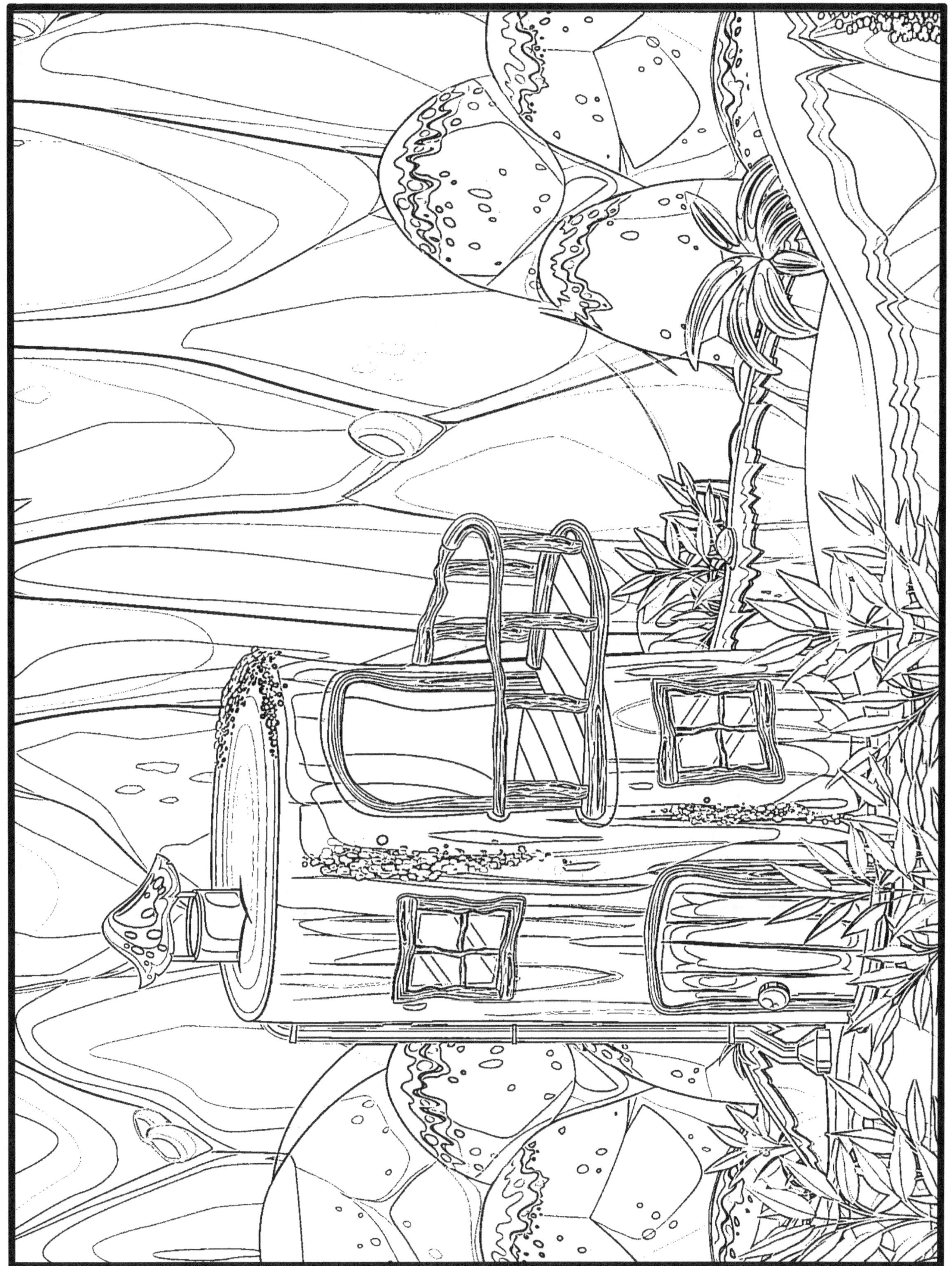

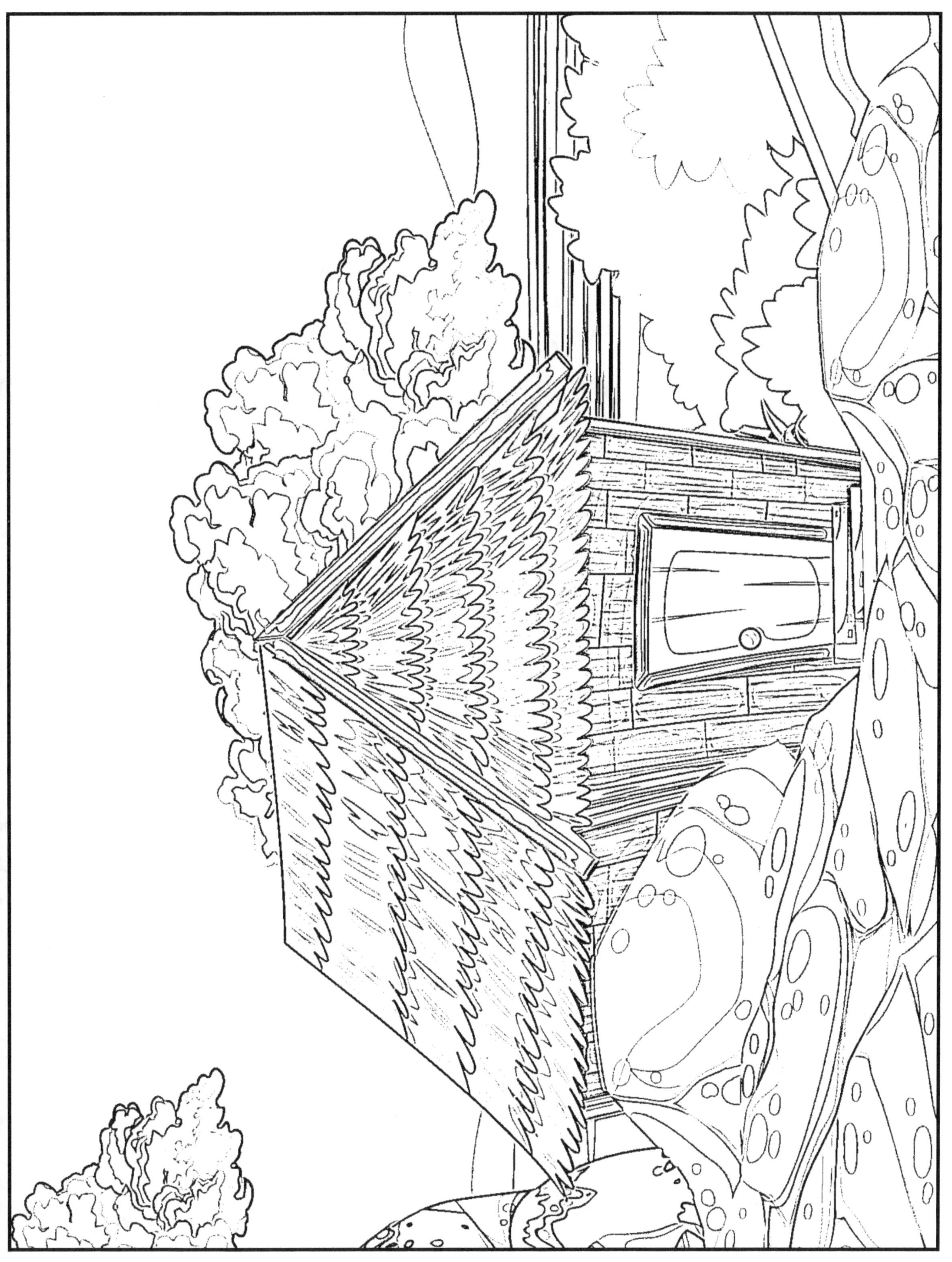

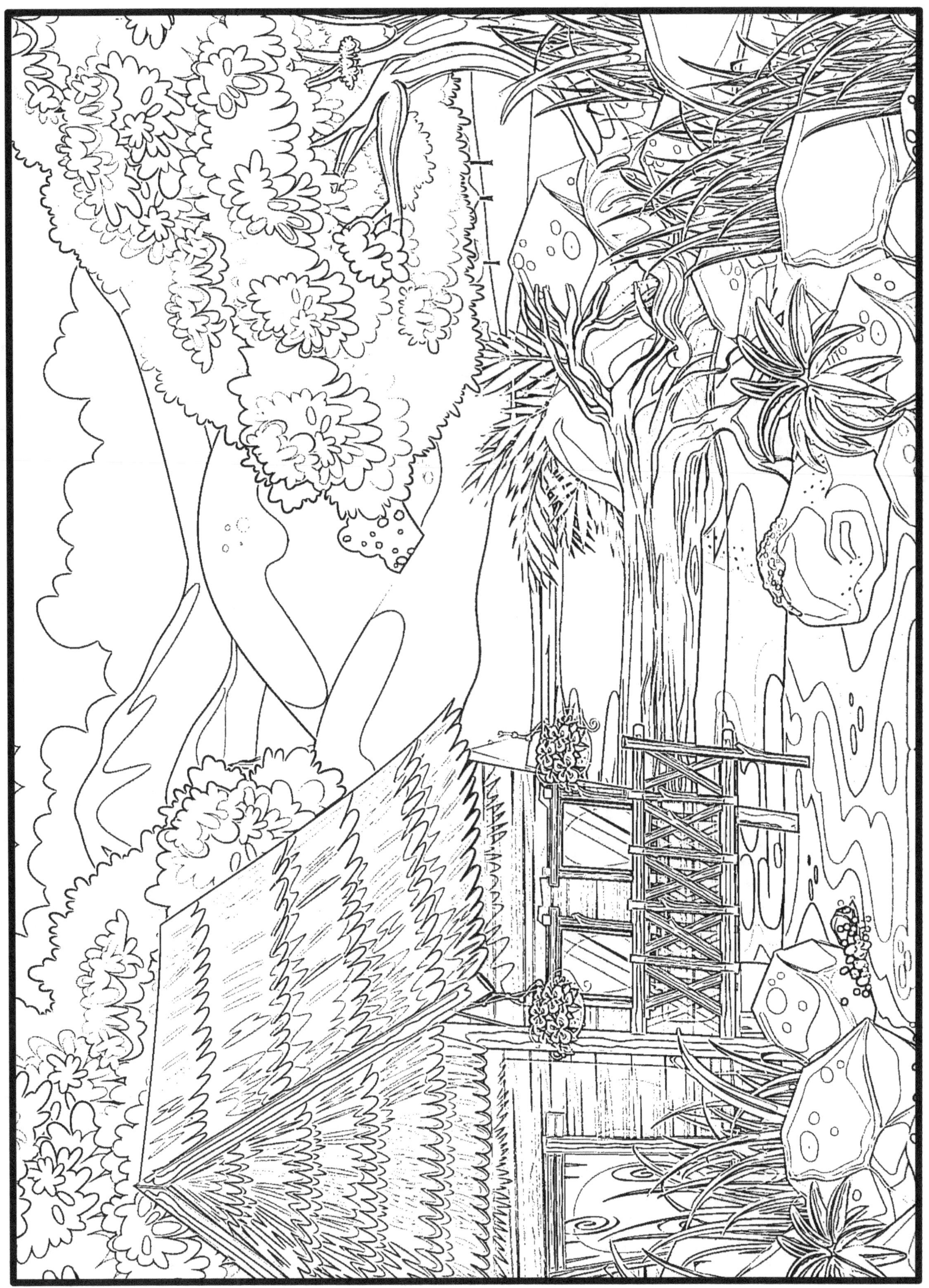

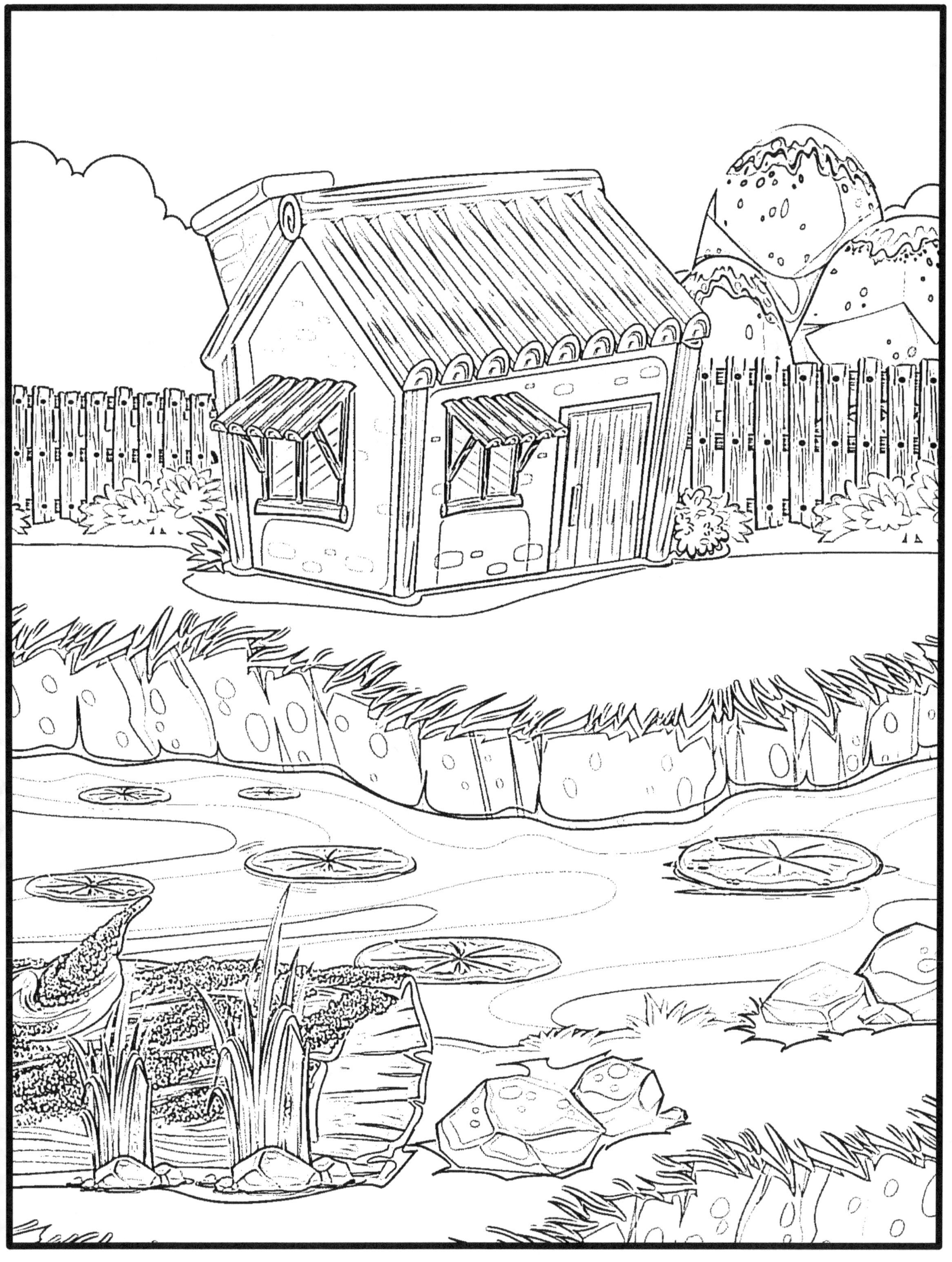

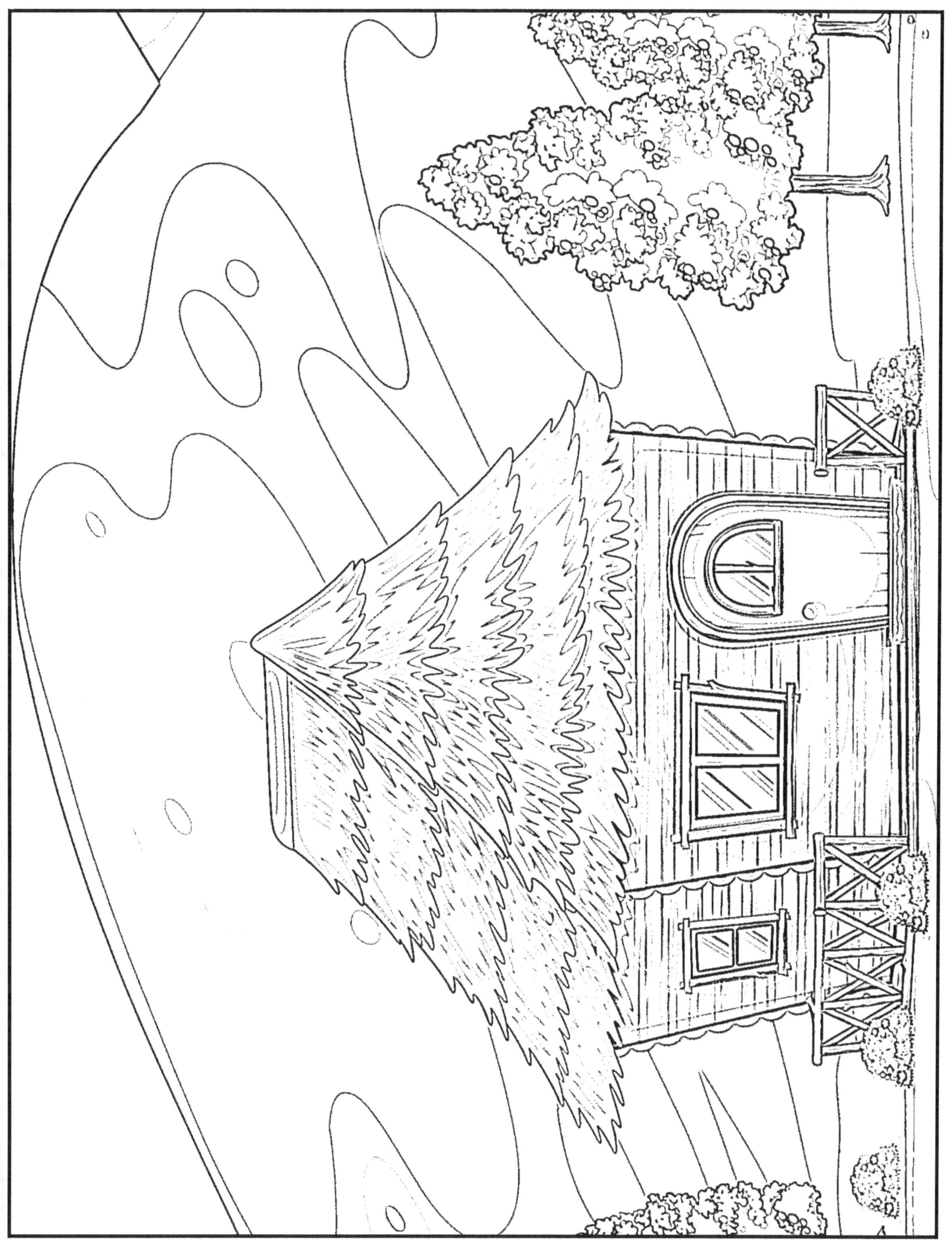

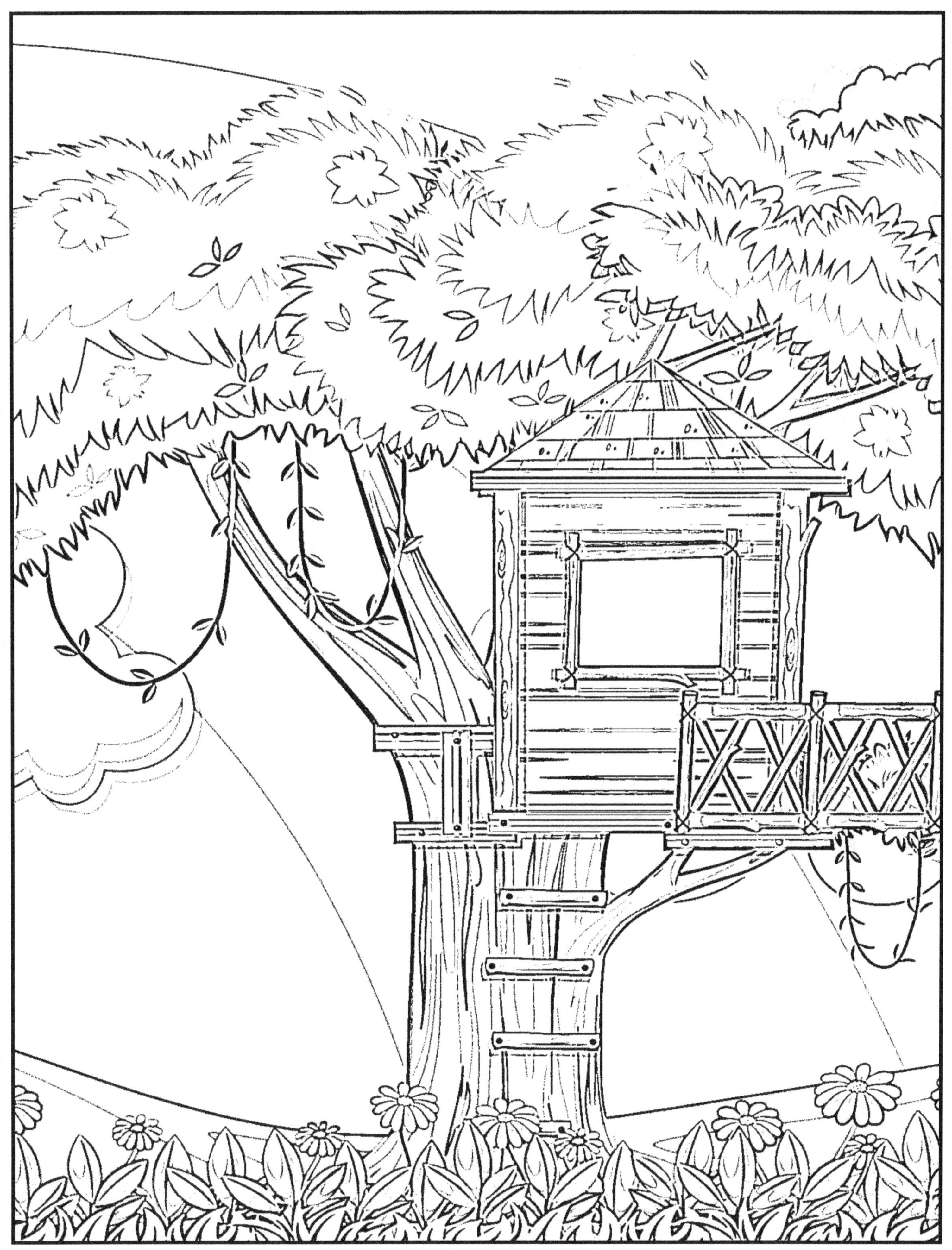

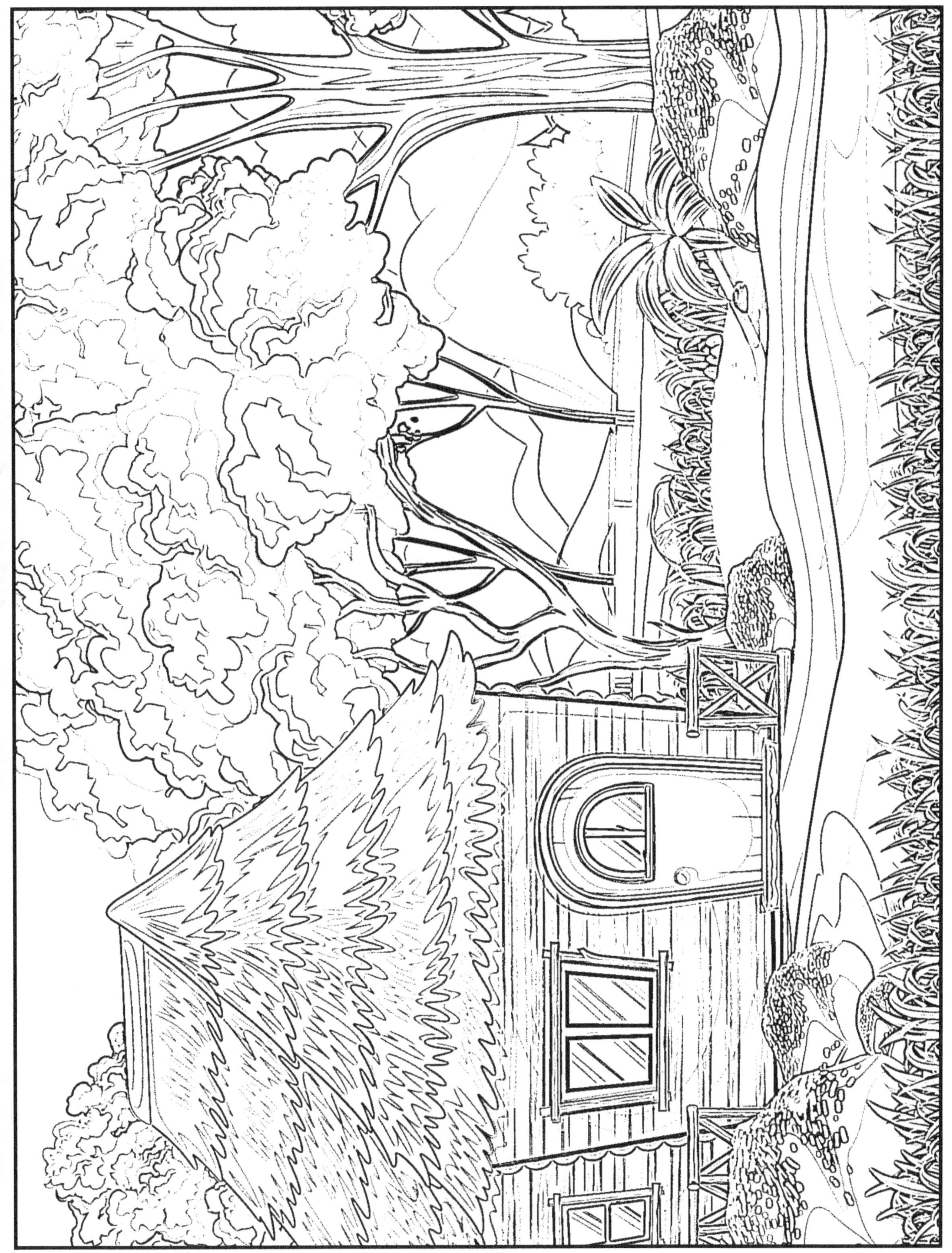

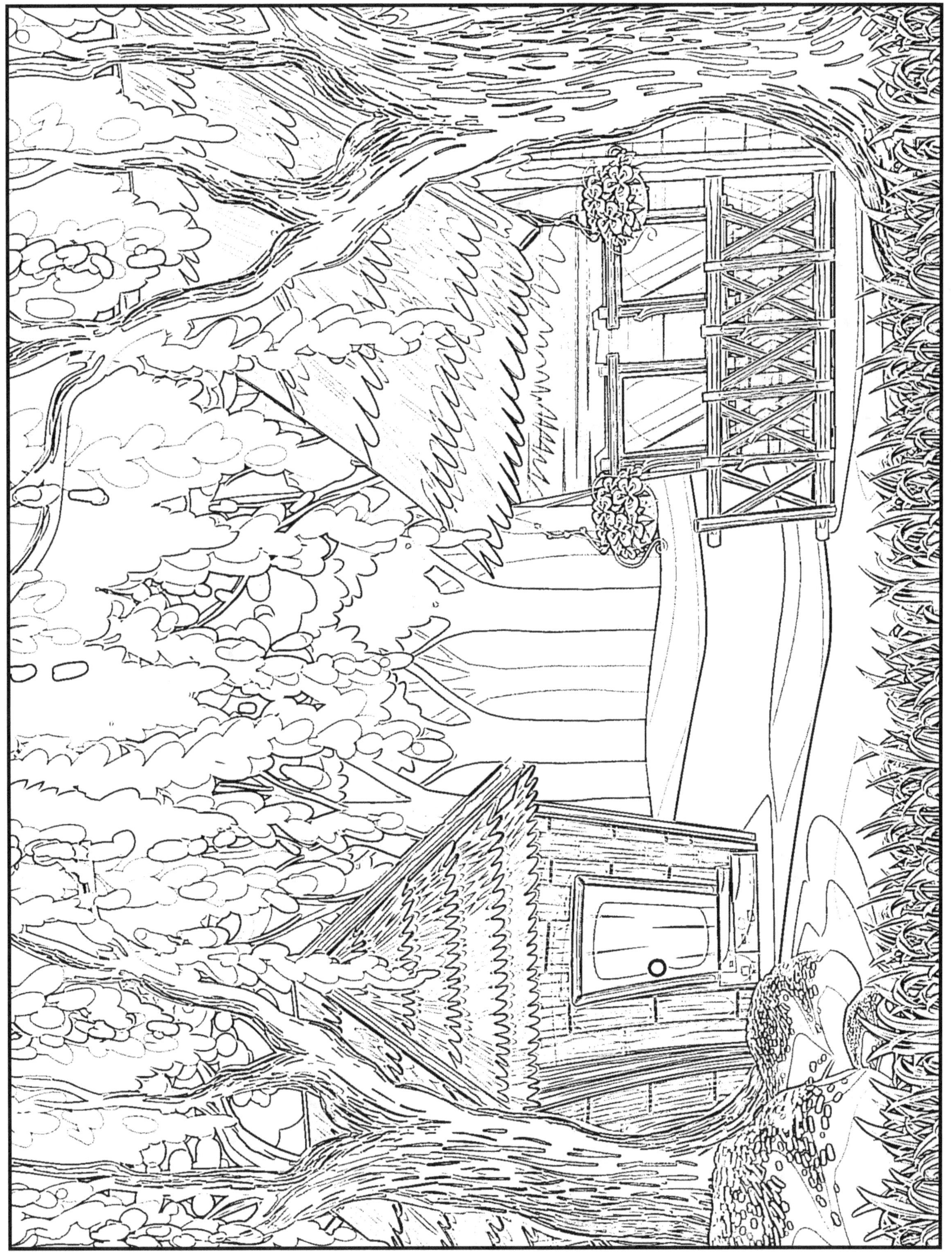